THE POWER OF
TRYING AGAIN

Featuring the story of Abraham Lincoln

Authors
Della Mae Rasmussen
Phyllis Colonna

Art Illustrator
Stephen P. Krause

Editor, Layout and Research
Beatrice W. Friel

THE POWER OF
TRYING AGAIN

Featuring the story of Abraham Lincoln

Advisors
Paul and Millie Cheesman
Mark Ray Davis
Rodney L. Mann, Jr.
Roxanne Shallenberger
Dale T. Tingey

Publisher
Steven R. Shallenberger

Director and Correlator
Lael J. Woodbury

AN EAGLE SYSTEMS
INTERNATIONAL
PUBLICATION

ANTIOCH, CALIFORNIA

The Power of Trying Again
Copyright © 1981 by
PowerTales
Eagle Systems International
P.O. Box 1229
Antioch, California 94509

ISBN: 0-911712-86-0

Library of Congress Catalog No.: 81-50389

First Edition

Lithographed in USA by
COMMUNITY PRESS, INC.

Dedicated to our youth, this story is about a man who
realized *the power of trying again.*

ABRAHAM LINCOLN

Abraham Lincoln was born 12 February 1809 on the Kentucky frontier to Thomas and Nancy Hanks Lincoln. The Lincolns, with their two-year-old daughter, Sarah, lived in a log cabin that had only one room and a dirt floor. When Abe was two, the family moved to Knob Creek, an area with clear streams, high hills, and magnificent cedar trees. There, in a small backwoods school, Abe and Sarah learned to read and write.

When Abe was seven, the family moved to a spot in Indiana about 16 miles from the Ohio River. During their first winter they lived in what was called a "half-faced camp"—a hastily built shed enclosed on three sides and open toward the south. They had to have a large campfire burning on the open side day and night to keep them warm and to ward off wild animals. However, within a few months the family was able to move into a log cabin built by Mr. Lincoln and Abe. It was here that Abe's mother died.

There followed a lonely, difficult time for the Lincoln family until 1819, when Abe's father remarried. He married Sarah Bush Johnston, a widow with three children. Abe's new stepmother was energetic and affectionate and took care of the Lincoln children as though they were her own. Abe became very fond of her.

Like other pioneer boys, Abe spent most of his time doing odd jobs about the farm. Whenever possible he attended school, walking four miles to school and another four miles home. He acquired most of his education by reading books on his own. He had a quick, inquiring mind. He borrowed and read all the books he could, and he loved to tell stories.

When Abe was 19, he left frontier life for the first time, taking a flatboat loaded with produce down the Ohio and Mississippi Rivers to New Orleans. Upon his return he worked in a store for a time and then moved with his family to Illinois. Later his family moved on, but Abe remained behind. Working as a storekeeper in New Salem, he studied in his spare time. Here he established a reputation for honesty, kindness, and reliability and here he first became involved in politics.

In 1832 Abe became a candidate for the Illinois state legislature, but was defeated. Persevering, he again ran in 1834 and this time he was elected. He served four consecutive terms. When the legislature was not in session, Abe studied law from borrowed books. In 1836 he received his license to practice law.

At the age of thirty-three, Abe married Mary Todd. They had four sons, Robert, Edward, William, and Thomas (Tad).

In 1846 he was elected to the U.S. House of Representatives. He served only one term and then returned to his law practice in Illinois, where he became a prominent lawyer. However, as slavery became a national political issue, Abe again became actively involved in politics. Condemning slavery as a "moral, social and political evil," he became a national figure. In November of 1860 Abe was elected President of the United States. On the way to his inauguration he said:

I now leave . . . with a task before me greater than that which rested upon Washington. Without the assistance of that Divine Being, who ever attended him, I cannot succeed. With that assistance I cannot fail.

During his first few weeks in office, Abe attempted to avoid war with the South. However, on 12 April 1861, Confederate batteries fired on Fort Sumter and the Civil War was begun. At this point Abe's primary objective was restoration of the Union. But by the summer of 1862 the slavery question had become a burning issue. Deciding for the freedom of slaves, President Lincoln issued the Emancipation Proclamation in January of 1863. In 1864 he was reelected to the presidency. General Lee surrendered on 9 April 1865. Abe's purpose had been accomplished: the Union was saved.

While the nation was still rejoicing, a great tragedy befell it. On 14 April 1865, at the age of fifty-six, Abe was shot while attending the theater. He died the next morning. It was said that the "whole nation, North and South, mourned his death with a deep, stunned sense of loss." Yet only after his death did people realize his true greatness. Without formal education, he had been one of the finest orators of his time and a great statesman. He had also been a man of kindness, infinite courage, and patience.

If someone asked you, "Who do you think was the greatest American that ever lived," what would you answer? Can you guess who most people name more often than any other person? Abraham Lincoln!

That makes me very happy because Abraham Lincoln has always been a special friend of mine. But let me introduce myself. My name is Barnaby Book. You may be wondering how Abe Lincoln came to be such a great American. I hope so, because that's a very interesting story. It's one I'd like to tell you.

Abe was born on a cold February morning in 1809—February 12, to be exact. His father and mother, Tom and Nancy Hanks Lincoln, lived on a farm near Hodgenville, Kentucky. Their rough log cabin had only one room, one window, and a big fireplace they used for heating the house and cooking their food.

Abe had a two-year-old sister named Sarah. He also had a cousin named Dennis Hanks who lived in a neighboring cabin two miles away. On this particular morning Dennis looked up from his breakfast to see his uncle standing in the doorway. "Nancy's got a baby boy," Tom Lincoln told Dennis' mother.

"Oh my! That's news I didn't expect to hear this soon!" Mrs. Hanks said. "I'd better hurry my work so I can go right over to help." But Dennis didn't want to waste even that much time. He ran the whole two miles to the Lincoln cabin.

When Mrs. Hanks finally arrived, Dennis watched her give the new baby his first bath. Then she dressed him in a warm flannel nightgown. "He's not very purty, is he?" Dennis asked his mother. "He looks like red cherry pulp squeezed dry."

"Hush now, Dennis!" Mrs. Hanks scolded. "You can't tell what folks are by how they look." Dennis didn't seem convinced, but in Abe's case what she said was very true. Even after he was grown up, he was not considered "good-looking." In fact, some folks said he was homely. But Abe Lincoln changed the course of American history.

11

After Mrs. Hanks handed the new baby back to his mother, she tidied up the cabin and cooked some dried berries for the rest of the family to eat. When she returned home that evening, Dennis stayed behind. He had been waiting for this cousin for a long time, and he wanted to keep an eye on him. He rolled up in a big bearskin and slept on the floor by the fireplace that night.

Abe grew fast—so fast that his mother could scarcely keep him in clothes. His pants and shirts always seemed too short for his arms and legs. Even when he was learning to walk, his father joked about his long legs. They always seemed to be tripping over something. But no matter how many times Abe fell down, he got right up again. "He's no quitter, that one," Tom Lincoln laughed. "He will try again no matter how many times it takes—just look at him!"

Although Dennis was a few years older than Abe, the two cousins became best friends. Dennis showed Abe how to fish in the creek and set traps for rabbits and muskrats. Sometimes the two boys followed Abe's father to the bee trees when he went to find wild honey.

The year Abe was four, Mr. and Mrs. Lincoln decided to move to Knob Creek, fifteen miles away. Abe was sad to live so far from Dennis, but soon something happened to take his mind off his loneliness. He started school. From the very first day he liked it very much. His teacher liked him, too. "Abe is very young, but he is a bright boy," she told Mrs. Lincoln. "He is making splendid progress in his studies. He never stops trying until he has mastered a problem."

Nancy Lincoln was proud of both Abe and Sarah. She helped them learn at home, too. Often they sat on her knee while she told the Bible stories, fairy tales, and country legends she had learned when she was a little girl. She taught Abe to gather spicewood bushes and put them on top of the burning log in the fireplace. "Spicewood makes a bright light to study by," she told him.

I guess you could say that's when Abe and I became such good friends. By the time he was seven years old, he was reading every book he could find. Sometimes he would walk for a day to borrow a new book he had heard about. Some of his favorites were *Robinson Crusoe*, *Aesop's Fables*, and *Pilgrim's Progress*. For the rest of his life Abe thought of a book as one of the best friends anyone could have.

The Lincolns didn't live in their new home for very many years. One day Mr. Lincoln said, "We have to move away from here, Nancy. Kentucky has decided to become a slave state."

"What is a slave state?" Abe asked his father.

"It's a state where one man can buy another man like a piece of furniture," his father answered. That was the first time Abe had ever heard that people could own other people. He could tell by his father's voice that having slaves was not a good thing.

Soon Mr. Lincoln moved his family to Pigeon Creek near Gentryville, Indiana. Abe was seven years old. His father said, "You're big enough to help build our cabin this time, son. Let me show you how to use an ax."

At first Abe thought he'd never be able to use it right. It was almost as heavy as he was, and the trees were so hard that the blade bounced off instead of cutting a chip. Abe was determined to show his father that he could work as well as anyone. He tried again and again until he could make the wood chips fly as fast as a grown man.

When Abe and Mr. Lincoln had enough logs ready, they put them together to make a new cabin. They built a loft above the big downstairs room. That is where Abe slept, on a pile of dry leaves covered with animal skins. Frontier life was hard, but Abe was learning to stay with a job until it was done.

Not long after the new home was finished, Abe had a wonderful surprise. Some neighbors started building a cabin not far away, and who should it be but the Hanks family and Abe's favorite cousin, Dennis! Soon the two boys were spending as much time together as they had before. They liked all the pioneer sports. Whenever they had a chance they went swimming or fishing, or they ran races or had wrestling contests. One day they went hunting wild turkeys. Abe shot one first thing, but then he was sad.

"I'm afraid you're too tenderhearted for your own good," Dennis told him.

"Maybe so," Abe answered. "But I wish I hadn't done that. I never want to pull the trigger on another living thing, unless I have to."

By this time Abe was one of the tallest boys in the area. All the hard work he did was making him very strong, too. One day his father said, "I need you to take the corn to the mill to grind. Can you do it without my help?" Abe said he thought he could, and soon he was on his way.

The boys at the mill liked to pass their time teasing, fighting, and looking for someone new to pick on. Abe had to wait a long time for the corn to be ground, so he stood back against a tree and watched. Several old men were outside enjoying the sunshine, and one of them said, "That's the shyest, homeliest, most awkward boy I've ever seen. He's the worst dressed, too. Those other boys will never leave him alone to mind his own business."

He was right. He had scarcely finished speaking when one big bully walked over to Abe and tried to shove him away from the tree. Soon all the other boys had jumped into the fight, too.

But Abe had learned not to give up just because the odds were agains him. Soon he had whipped the first two boys who jumped on him and was finishing up the third. then he leaned back against the tree and shouted, "Does anyone else want a taste of it, too?" No one else did, or at least no one ventured out to tell him so. All the people near Gentryville began to talk with respect about this determined boy who was both strong and gentle.

THINK ABOUT IT

1. Can you think of some times when Abe tried and tried again?
2. How did Abe get ready to be a leader of his country?

26

CHANGES COME INTO ABE'S LIFE

The year Abe was nine, a great sadness came into his life. His mother became very ill. One day she called her two children to her bedside. "Live as I have always taught you," she told them weakly. "Love your family and worship God." She put her hand on Abe's head and whispered, "Be kind and good to your father and your sister."

It was a sad and lonely time for all the family after Nancy Lincoln died. Sarah was only eleven, but she did her best to cook the meals and keep the cabin clean. One night Mr. Lincoln lay awake thinking. "It has been a year since we lost Nancy. The children are sad—all the happiness seems gone from our poor home. I can't be both mother and father to them."

Back in Kentucky lived a widow named Sarah Bush Johnston. Mr. Lincoln had known her for many years. Next morning he said to Abe and Sarah, "You two take care of each other. I have to travel to Kentucky for a time."

He went straight to the home of Sarah Johnston. He said, "Sarah, I am a lone man, and you are a lone woman. I have known you from a girl, and you have known me. I've come all the way from Indiana to ask if you'll marry me."

Sarah answered, "Tommy Lincoln, I have no objection to marrying, but I owe several little debts which must be paid first." Mr. Lincoln paid the debts that same evening, and the next day they were married. Then they packed up Sarah's belongings and, with her three children, started back to Indiana.

It was a glorious day for Abe and Sarah when this strong, cheerful woman came to their home. She took them into her arms, and they felt the first warmth and hope they had known in a long time.

Their new mother had a fine collection of furniture and household goods, and she set right to work making a comfortable home. Abe and Sarah had never seen such wealth. She even had feather beds for all the family, and for the first time Abe had more than a pile of leaves to sleep on. Between the children and their new mother grew a love that was to last all their lives.

Abe's stepmother helped him with his studies at home just as his real mother had. She encouraged him to read as much as he could. "Don't worry!" he laughed. "I would like to read every book there is. The things I want to know are found in books.

Mrs. Lincoln said to Abe's father, "I have never seen the likes of that boy—his intelligence, his honesty, his determination. Someday he will be someone special."

Abe wanted to be someone special. He thought people should aim high and then keep trying until they reached their goals. One day he was shucking corn for Mrs. Crawford, one of the neighbors. While he worked, he talked.

"You know, Mrs. Crawford, I'm not going to spend all my life shucking corn and splitting rails. I'm going to fit myself for a profession," he said.

"And what do you want to be now?" Mrs. Crawford asked him.

"Someday I'll be President," Abe answered.

Mrs. Crawford knew Abe liked to tease. "You'd make a purty president, with all your jokes and tricks, wouldn't you?" she said.

But this time Abe was serious. "Oh, I'll study and get ready," he answered. "Then when the chance comes, I'll find a way to take it."

Abe was good at finding ways to do things. He made his own ink from brier roots, and his pen was cut from a buzzard quill. He wrote his arithmetic problems on the bottom of the wooden fire shovel with a piece of charcoal. When the shovel bottom was covered with numbers, he shaved it off white and clean again.

Often he studied by the light of the fireplace until late at night, but he was always up again at dawn the next morning. He took a book with him while he worked, and whenever he had a spare minute he perched on a stump or a fence rail to read. "Look at that boy yonder and mark my words," he heard a father tell his son. "He will make a smart man out of himself."

By the time Abe was nineteen, he was six feet two inches tall and weighed 150 pounds. "That Abe Lincoln is the equal of three men!" one neighbor said. "He can sink an ax deeper into wood than any man I ever saw."

"I've seen him lift and carry two heavy logs single-handed," another added.

Abe was popular in the settlement because he was good-natured and interesting to talk to. He didn't like it when people tried to talk in such a fancy way that no one could understand them, so he learned to explain hard ideas in a clear and simple way. He also had a lively way of telling stories and a good sense of humor. "My father taught me to work hard," he joked one day, "but he never taught me to love it."

In 1828, the year before Abe was twenty, Mr. Gentry asked him to go on a Mississippi flatboat with his son Allen to trade bacon, corn, and other products in New Orleans. The boys thought the trip was great fun. One night they tied the flatboat against a landing and went to sleep in the tiny cabin as usual. Suddenly Allen opened his eyes and listened intently. He could hear footsteps on the deck. He knew a gang of thieves had slipped on board and wouldn't think twice about killing him and Abe and throwing them into the river.

"Quick, Abe, bring the guns!" Allen shouted so the thieves would think they were armed. "Shoot them!" The thieves laughed. They weren't the least bit afraid. But suddenly Abe was in the middle of them—not with a gun, but with a big club. Knocking thieves out of the way was nothing to someone who was used to chopping down trees all day.

The gang ran away as fast as they could scramble off that boat. Abe carried a white scar above his eye for the rest of his life to remind him of the adventure. Mr. Gentry told everyone, "Abe is the man to choose if you need a hard job done right!"

In 1830 Abe turned twenty-one. The Lincoln family decided to leave Indiana and move to New Salem, Illinois. Abe walked by the wagon in his buckskins and coonskin cap directing the oxen. He had a little dog that ran along beside him. One day, after crossing a swift stream, Abe noticed the dog was missing. He looked back and saw him whining on the other side of the river. The water was pouring over broken chunks of ice, and the poor animal was afraid to cross.

"Come on, Abe," his father said. "We can't hold up a whole party for one foolish animal." But Abe felt he couldn't abandon the little dog. He pulled off his shoes and waded back to rescue him. The grateful animal jumped with joy, licking Abe's face and hands whenever he could reach them. "I reckon that's reward enough for cold feet," Abe said.

In Illinois the family chose a hill overlooking the Sagamon River and built another cabin. Once again Abe split rails, built fences, and broke prairie ground to plant crops. His jokes and good humor soon won him many friends in Sagamon.

In the spring of 1830 he and several other men took a boatload of corn and hogs downriver to New Orleans. They reached the city in early May, and for the first time Abe saw for himself the misery of slavery. He saw human beings whipped, chained, and sold to the highest bidder. He saw black families separated, one member sold to one buyer and another sold to someone else.

"Boys, let's get away from this," he said to his friends. "If I ever get a chance to hit at slavery, I'll hit it hard."

When Abe returned to Illinois, he worked for a while in a store. Then he decided to go into politics. He liked to study history and law, and he liked to give speeches and argue his ideas in the country stores.

THINK ABOUT IT

1. What are some of the things you like best about Abe Lincoln?
2. What goals do you have for your life? What things do you need to do to prepare yourself?

44

ABE GOES INTO POLITICS

"I've decided to run as a candidate for the state legislature," he told his father. "I want a say in how the state is run, and I'll take my case to the people. If they decide against me, I won't be greatly disappointed. I'm already familiar with disappointment." When disappointments came to Abe, he had learned to wait for a better moment, then try again.

He had scarcely begun his campaign when the Black Hawk War broke out, and the governor called for volunteers to fight the Indians. Abe stepped forward along with the other boys from his neighborhood. They elected him their captain, and he had his first experience governing other men. It wasn't an easy task because these men didn't much like being governed! Once he had to stand against everybody in his outfit because they wanted to kill a friendly Indian who was seeking refuge at their camp.

When the war ended, Abe went back to New Salem. He had to earn a living, so he and a man named Mr. Berry decided to be partners in the grocery store business. They borrowed money to buy the only three grocery stores in town, but they weren't good businessmen. Mr. Berry spent most of his time drinking, and Abe couldn't seem to quit reading and studying. Their business failed, and a short time later Mr. Berry died. That left Abe to pay off more than a thousand dollars the two men had borrowed. It seemed like so much money that Abe called it the national debt. It took him many years, but he finally paid off every cent. People began to call him Honest Abe, and in 1834 they elected him to the Illinois state legislature.

When Abe was twenty-five he fell in love with a beautiful, gentle girl named Ann Rutledge. Ann had auburn hair and blue eyes, and she was interested in books, people, and all the things Abe was interested in. They spent a glorious summer going on buggy rides, picnics, and dances. They decided to get married as soon as Abe finished his law studies, but in August 1835 Ann became very ill. A short time later she died, and Abe fell into such a deep grief that his friends were afraid he might die too.

"You can't give up because Ann is gone," they told him. "Now you must work twice as hard to do all the things you and Ann talked about doing." Abe knew they were right, so he went back to his studies. In 1836 he passed his exams and was ready to practice law.

That same year he was reelected to the Illinois legislature. He moved to
Springfield and soon he had as many friends in the state capital as he had
in all the other places he had lived. He still had the reputation of being
honest, wise, gentle, and kind.

One day Abe was riding his horse along a country road with several men from the legislature. He saw two little birds that had fallen from their nest. They weren't old enough to fly, and the mother bird was fluttering around and chirping with distress. Abe stopped and tied up his horse. He picked up the little birds and climbed the tree to put them back in their nest. His friends laughed at him, but he said: "Gentlemen, I could not have slept well tonight if I had not saved those birds. Their cries would have rung in my ears."

Abe was becoming more and more concerned with the question of slavery. In 1838 he was elected to the legislature again, but he was defeated as Speaker of the House. In 1840 he was once more defeated as Speaker of the House. "Never mind," he said with a smile. "In two years I'll try again."

It was about this time that Abe met a man who would be his competitor for the rest of his life. The man's name was Stephen Douglas, and he and Abe even fell in love with the same girl.

Mary Todd from Kentucky had come to Springfield to visit relatives. She was attractive and well-educated, and she was very ambitious. Once she had vowed that someday she would be the wife of the President of the United States. Many people thought Mary would choose the dashing, clever Stephen Douglas over the big, awkward Lincoln, but they were surprised. Mary made her choice, and on November 4, 1842, she and Abe were married.

Mary Todd Lincoln was a gracious hostess. She knew how to entertain people in a way that made them feel important. At first she and Abe lived in a little inn, but Mary wanted a house of her own. "We need a real home with nice furniture and lace curtains," she said. Abe agreed, and soon they found just the house they wanted. Three sons were born to them in the years they lived there.

Abe adored his sons and often took them with him to work. His long legs would stride along the streets of Springfield while one of his little boys tugged at his hand or hurried to keep up. Abe was a very clean man, but he was not orderly. His office was crowded with stacks of books and stacks of papers. He carried most of his legal documents in his tall stovepipe hat. People said he was one of the best lawyers in Illinois.

In 1846 Abe was elected to the Congress of the United States and moved to Washington, D.C. He always voted for what he thought was right, even when other people didn't agree with him. "You'd better be careful what you say," Mary told him one day. "Some people think you are too outspoken."

"I can only vote for the truth," Abe said. "You wouldn't have me vote for a lie."

Some people did think Abe was too outspoken, and in the next election he was defeated. In 1854 he was defeated again.

"I think maybe you'd better just stay home and practice law," one of his friends told him.

"No," Abe answered, "the struggle has just begun. I will try again."

For many years he and Stephen Douglas had been on opposite sides of the slavery question. Stephen Douglas gave many speeches, saying, "Every state should choose whether to have slaves or not." But every time Stephen Douglas gave a speech, Abe gave one too. He said, "No man is good enough to govern another man without his consent. This nation cannot endure half slave and half free."

In 1858 Abe and Stephen Douglas both ran for election to the United States Senate. They began to hold public debates. Thousands of people came to hear them each time they spoke. Stephen Douglas gave all the reasons why people should have slaves if they wanted to. Abe asked the question, "Is slavery right, or wrong?" He thought all the people knew in their hearts that it was wrong. Abe lost the election by a few votes and was terribly disappointed. "I feel like the boy that stubbed his toe," he said. "It hurt too bad to laugh, but he was too big to cry."

Even though Abe lost the election, the people of the United States had heard him speak, and they liked his ideas. They asked him to give more speeches. In 1860 he was nominated for President of the United States. Once again his opponent was Stephen Douglas, but this time Abe won. Cannons boomed out the good news on the night of the election.

Abe had lost many elections in the thirty years he had been in politics, but he always got up and tried again. Now he had won the highest office in the land. You might think he had won his greatest victory, but he found that his hardest struggles had not yet begun.

Soon after the election many southern states began to leave the Union. The Civil War had started. It lasted four long, terrible years. The man who didn't even want to shoot a wild turkey had to watch thousands of soldiers die to settle the slavery question. He often visited their camps, sometimes with his little son Tad at his side. After one terrible battle he gave one of the most famous speeches in American history: the Gettysburg Address.

In 1863 he signed the Emancipation Proclamation, giving all the slaves their freedom. Still the South kept fighting. "I've got to find a way to end this war," Abe said. "I've tried every way I can think of, but I've got to try something more."

Finally he found a general he thought could lead the North to victory—General Ulysses S. Grant. In 1865 Grant's army captured the Southern capital Richmond, Virginia, and the war was over at last. Abe had succeeded in the hardest task he had ever tried to do. The slaves were free. The Union was saved.

Abe asked the band to play "Dixie," the favorite song of the South. "Can't we join together once again in a spirit of kindness and forgiveness?" he asked. But not everyone was as wise and kind as he was.

On April 14, 1865, he went to a play at Ford's theater. He liked the show, and he laughed and joked with the people in the presidential box. But suddenly a pistol shot rang out. A woman began to scream. "They have shot the President!" she cried. Everything was in confusion. The murderer, John Wilkes Booth, jumped to the stage and ran off into the night.

Abe was carried to a nearby apartment. His wife and friends stayed with him all through the night, but he died without regaining consciousness. A man standing by his bedside said quietly, "Now he belongs to the ages."

Abe would be glad to know he is still remembered more than a hundred years after his death. He would be glad that his work is being carried on by others. Perhaps that is why so many people think he is one of the greatest Americans who ever lived. He tried to be wise, strong, and kind, and that is what America tries to be. Abe taught us all to aim high and then keep trying until we reach our goals.